Ozymandias an

By Percy Bysshe Shelley

Includes MLA Style Citations for
Scholarly Secondary Sources,
Peer-Reviewed Journal Articles
and Critical Essays

Squid Ink Classics

HAPPY BiRthdAy !

MARCH 2019

TO: MOM

LOVE,

GRACE

Ozymandias and Other Poems

By Percy Bysshe Shelley

Includes MLA Style Citations for Scholarly Secondary Sources, Peer-Reviewed Journal Articles and Critical Essays

Squid Ink Classics

Library of Congress Cataloging in Publication Data

Squid Ink Classics

ISBN-13:

978-1979338356

ISBN-10:

1979338353

Published by Squid Ink Classics

Boston, Massachusetts

Ozymandias and Other Poems

By Percy Bysshe Shelley

Ozymandias

I met a traveller from an antique land,

Who said—"Two vast and trunkless legs of stone

Stand in the desert. . . . Near them, on the sand,

Half sunk a shattered visage lies, whose frown,

And wrinkled lip, and sneer of cold command,

Tell that its sculptor well those passions read

Which yet survive, stamped on these lifeless things,

The hand that mocked them, and the heart that fed;

And on the pedestal, these words appear:

My name is Ozymandias, King of Kings;

Look on my Works, ye Mighty, and despair!

Nothing beside remains. Round the decay

Of that colossal Wreck, boundless and bare

The lone and level sands stretch far away."

my favorit poem

Ode to the West Wind

I

O wild West Wind, thou breath of Autumn's being,

Thou, from whose unseen presence the leaves dead

Are driven, like ghosts from an enchanter fleeing,

Yellow, and black, and pale, and hectic red,

Pestilence-stricken multitudes: O thou,

Who chariotest to their dark wintry bed

The winged seeds, where they lie cold and low,

Each like a corpse within its grave, until

Thine azure sister of the Spring shall blow

Her clarion o'er the dreaming earth, and fill

(Driving sweet buds like flocks to feed in air)

With living hues and odours plain and hill:

Wild Spirit, which art moving everywhere;

Destroyer and preserver; hear, oh hear!

II

Thou on whose stream, mid the steep sky's commotion,

Loose clouds like earth's decaying leaves are shed,

Shook from the tangled boughs of Heaven and Ocean,

Angels of rain and lightning: there are spread

On the blue surface of thine aëry surge,

Like the bright hair uplifted from the head

Of some fierce Maenad, even from the dim verge

Of the horizon to the zenith's height,

The locks of the approaching storm. Thou dirge

Of the dying year, to which this closing night

Will be the dome of a vast sepulchre,

Vaulted with all thy congregated might

Of vapours, from whose solid atmosphere

Black rain, and fire, and hail will burst: oh hear!

III

Thou who didst waken from his summer dreams

The blue Mediterranean, where he lay,

Lull'd by the coil of his crystalline streams,

Beside a pumice isle in Baiae's bay,

And saw in sleep old palaces and towers

Quivering within the wave's intenser day,

All overgrown with azure moss and flowers

So sweet, the sense faints picturing them! Thou

For whose path the Atlantic's level powers

Cleave themselves into chasms, while far below

The sea-blooms and the oozy woods which wear

The sapless foliage of the ocean, know

Thy voice, and suddenly grow gray with fear,

And tremble and despoil themselves: oh hear!

IV

If I were a dead leaf thou mightest bear;

If I were a swift cloud to fly with thee;

A wave to pant beneath thy power, and share

The impulse of thy strength, only less free

Than thou, O uncontrollable! If even

I were as in my boyhood, and could be

The comrade of thy wanderings over Heaven,

As then, when to outstrip thy skiey speed

Scarce seem'd a vision; I would ne'er have striven

As thus with thee in prayer in my sore need.

Oh, lift me as a wave, a leaf, a cloud!

I fall upon the thorns of life! I bleed!

A heavy weight of hours has chain'd and bow'd

One too like thee: tameless, and swift, and proud.

V

Make me thy lyre, even as the forest is:

What if my leaves are falling like its own!

The tumult of thy mighty harmonies

Will take from both a deep, autumnal tone,

Sweet though in sadness. Be thou, Spirit fierce,

My spirit! Be thou me, impetuous one!

Drive my dead thoughts over the universe

Like wither'd leaves to quicken a new birth!

And, by the incantation of this verse,

Scatter, as from an unextinguish'd hearth

Ashes and sparks, my words among mankind!

Be through my lips to unawaken'd earth

The trumpet of a prophecy! O Wind,

If Winter comes, can Spring be far behind?

Adonais: An Elegy on the Death of John Keats

I

I weep for Adonais—he is dead!

Oh, weep for Adonais! though our tears

Thaw not the frost which binds so dear a head!

And thou, sad Hour, selected from all years

To mourn our loss, rouse thy obscure compeers,

And teach them thine own sorrow, say: "With me

Died Adonais; till the Future dares

Forget the Past, his fate and fame shall be

An echo and a light unto eternity!"

II

Where wert thou, mighty Mother, when he lay,

When thy Son lay, pierc'd by the shaft which flies

In darkness? where was lorn Urania

When Adonais died? With veiled eyes,

'Mid listening Echoes, in her Paradise

She sate, while one, with soft enamour'd breath,

Rekindled all the fading melodies,

With which, like flowers that mock the corse beneath,

He had adorn'd and hid the coming bulk of Death.

III

Oh, weep for Adonais—he is dead!

Wake, melancholy Mother, wake and weep!

Yet wherefore? Quench within their burning bed

Thy fiery tears, and let thy loud heart keep

Like his, a mute and uncomplaining sleep;

For he is gone, where all things wise and fair

Descend—oh, dream not that the amorous Deep

Will yet restore him to the vital air;

Death feeds on his mute voice, and laughs at our despair.

IV

Most musical of mourners, weep again!

Lament anew, Urania! He died,

Who was the Sire of an immortal strain,

Blind, old and lonely, when his country's pride,

The priest, the slave and the liberticide,

Trampled and mock'd with many a loathed rite

Of lust and blood; he went, unterrified,

Into the gulf of death; but his clear Sprite

Yet reigns o'er earth; the third among the sons of light.

V

Most musical of mourners, weep anew!

Not all to that bright station dar'd to climb;

And happier they their happiness who knew,

Whose tapers yet burn through that night of time

In which suns perish'd; others more sublime,

Struck by the envious wrath of man or god,

Have sunk, extinct in their refulgent prime;

And some yet live, treading the thorny road,

Which leads, through toil and hate, to Fame's serene abode.

VI

But now, thy youngest, dearest one, has perish'd,

The nursling of thy widowhood, who grew,

Like a pale flower by some sad maiden cherish'd,

And fed with true-love tears, instead of dew;

Most musical of mourners, weep anew!

Thy extreme hope, the loveliest and the last,

The bloom, whose petals nipp'd before they blew

Died on the promise of the fruit, is waste;

The broken lily lies—the storm is overpast.

VII

To that high Capital, where kingly Death

Keeps his pale court in beauty and decay,

He came; and bought, with price of purest breath,

A grave among the eternal.—Come away!

Haste, while the vault of blue Italian day

Is yet his fitting charnel-roof! while still

He lies, as if in dewy sleep he lay;

Awake him not! surely he takes his fill

Of deep and liquid rest, forgetful of all ill.

VIII

He will awake no more, oh, never more!

Within the twilight chamber spreads apace

The shadow of white Death, and at the door

Invisible Corruption waits to trace

His extreme way to her dim dwelling-place;

The eternal Hunger sits, but pity and awe

Soothe her pale rage, nor dares she to deface

So fair a prey, till darkness and the law

Of change shall o'er his sleep the mortal curtain draw.

IX

Oh, weep for Adonais! The quick Dreams,

The passion-winged Ministers of thought,

Who were his flocks, whom near the living streams

Of his young spirit he fed, and whom he taught

The love which was its music, wander not—

Wander no more, from kindling brain to brain,

But droop there, whence they sprung; and mourn their lot

Round the cold heart, where, after their sweet pain,

They ne'er will gather strength, or find a home again.

X

And one with trembling hands clasps his cold head,

And fans him with her moonlight wings, and cries,

"Our love, our hope, our sorrow, is not dead;

See, on the silken fringe of his faint eyes,

Like dew upon a sleeping flower, there lies

A tear some Dream has loosen'd from his brain."

Lost Angel of a ruin'd Paradise!

She knew not 'twas her own; as with no stain

She faded, like a cloud which had outwept its rain.

XI

One from a lucid urn of starry dew

Wash'd his light limbs as if embalming them;

Another clipp'd her profuse locks, and threw

The wreath upon him, like an anadem,

Which frozen tears instead of pearls begem;

Another in her wilful grief would break

Her bow and winged reeds, as if to stem

A greater loss with one which was more weak;

And dull the barbed fire against his frozen cheek.

XII

Another Splendour on his mouth alit,

That mouth, whence it was wont to draw the breath

Which gave it strength to pierce the guarded wit,

And pass into the panting heart beneath

With lightning and with music: the damp death

Quench'd its caress upon his icy lips;

And, as a dying meteor stains a wreath

Of moonlight vapour, which the cold night clips,

It flush'd through his pale limbs, and pass'd to its eclipse.

XIII

And others came . . . Desires and Adorations,

Winged Persuasions and veil'd Destinies,

Splendours, and Glooms, and glimmering Incarnations

Of hopes and fears, and twilight Phantasies;

And Sorrow, with her family of Sighs,

And Pleasure, blind with tears, led by the gleam

Of her own dying smile instead of eyes,

Came in slow pomp; the moving pomp might seem

Like pageantry of mist on an autumnal stream.

XIV

All he had lov'd, and moulded into thought,

From shape, and hue, and odour, and sweet sound,

Lamented Adonais. Morning sought

Her eastern watch-tower, and her hair unbound,

Wet with the tears which should adorn the ground,

Dimm'd the aëreal eyes that kindle day;

Afar the melancholy thunder moan'd,

Pale Ocean in unquiet slumber lay,

And the wild Winds flew round, sobbing in their dismay.

XV

Lost Echo sits amid the voiceless mountains,

And feeds her grief with his remember'd lay,

And will no more reply to winds or fountains,

Or amorous birds perch'd on the young green spray,

Or herdsman's horn, or bell at closing day;

Since she can mimic not his lips, more dear

Than those for whose disdain she pin'd away

Into a shadow of all sounds: a drear

Murmur, between their songs, is all the woodmen hear.

XVI

Grief made the young Spring wild, and she threw down

Her kindling buds, as if she Autumn were,

Or they dead leaves; since her delight is flown,

For whom should she have wak'd the sullen year?

To Phoebus was not Hyacinth so dear

Nor to himself Narcissus, as to both

Thou, Adonais: wan they stand and sere

Amid the faint companions of their youth,

With dew all turn'd to tears; odour, to sighing ruth.

XVII

Thy spirit's sister, the lorn nightingale

Mourns not her mate with such melodious pain;

Not so the eagle, who like thee could scale

Heaven, and could nourish in the sun's domain

Her mighty youth with morning, doth complain,

Soaring and screaming round her empty nest,

As Albion wails for thee: the curse of Cain

Light on his head who pierc'd thy innocent breast,

And scar'd the angel soul that was its earthly guest!

XVIII

Ah, woe is me! Winter is come and gone,

But grief returns with the revolving year;

The airs and streams renew their joyous tone;

The ants, the bees, the swallows reappear;

Fresh leaves and flowers deck the dead Seasons' bier;

The amorous birds now pair in every brake,

And build their mossy homes in field and brere;

And the green lizard, and the golden snake,

Like unimprison'd flames, out of their trance awake.

XIX

Through wood and stream and field and hill and Ocean

A quickening life from the Earth's heart has burst

As it has ever done, with change and motion,

From the great morning of the world when first

God dawn'd on Chaos; in its stream immers'd,

The lamps of Heaven flash with a softer light;

All baser things pant with life's sacred thirst;

Diffuse themselves; and spend in love's delight,

The beauty and the joy of their renewed might.

XX

The leprous corpse, touch'd by this spirit tender,

Exhales itself in flowers of gentle breath;

Like incarnations of the stars, when splendour

Is chang'd to fragrance, they illumine death

And mock the merry worm that wakes beneath;

Nought we know, dies. Shall that alone which knows

Be as a sword consum'd before the sheath

By sightless lightning?—the intense atom glows

A moment, then is quench'd in a most cold repose.

XXI

Alas! that all we lov'd of him should be,

But for our grief, as if it had not been,

And grief itself be mortal! Woe is me!

Whence are we, and why are we? of what scene

The actors or spectators? Great and mean

Meet mass'd in death, who lends what life must borrow.

As long as skies are blue, and fields are green,

Evening must usher night, night urge the morrow,

Month follow month with woe, and year wake year to sorrow.

XXII

He will awake no more, oh, never more!

"Wake thou," cried Misery, "childless Mother, rise

Out of thy sleep, and slake, in thy heart's core,

A wound more fierce than his, with tears and sighs."

And all the Dreams that watch'd Urania's eyes,

And all the Echoes whom their sister's song

Had held in holy silence, cried: "Arise!"

Swift as a Thought by the snake Memory stung,

From her ambrosial rest the fading Splendour sprung.

XXIII

She rose like an autumnal Night, that springs

Out of the East, and follows wild and drear

The golden Day, which, on eternal wings,

Even as a ghost abandoning a bier,

Had left the Earth a corpse. Sorrow and fear

So struck, so rous'd, so rapt Urania;

So sadden'd round her like an atmosphere

Of stormy mist; so swept her on her way

Even to the mournful place where Adonais lay.

XXIV

Out of her secret Paradise she sped,

Through camps and cities rough with stone, and steel,

And human hearts, which to her aery tread

Yielding not, wounded the invisible

Palms of her tender feet where'er they fell:

And barbed tongues, and thoughts more sharp than they,

Rent the soft Form they never could repel,

Whose sacred blood, like the young tears of May,

Pav'd with eternal flowers that undeserving way.

XXV

In the death-chamber for a moment Death,

Sham'd by the presence of that living Might,

Blush'd to annihilation, and the breath

Revisited those lips, and Life's pale light

Flash'd through those limbs, so late her dear delight.

"Leave me not wild and drear and comfortless,

As silent lightning leaves the starless night!

Leave me not!" cried Urania: her distress

Rous'd Death: Death rose and smil'd, and met her vain caress.

XXVI

"Stay yet awhile! speak to me once again;

Kiss me, so long but as a kiss may live;

And in my heartless breast and burning brain

That word, that kiss, shall all thoughts else survive,

With food of saddest memory kept alive,

Now thou art dead, as if it were a part

Of thee, my Adonais! I would give

All that I am to be as thou now art!

But I am chain'd to Time, and cannot thence depart!

XXVII

"O gentle child, beautiful as thou wert,

Why didst thou leave the trodden paths of men

Too soon, and with weak hands though mighty heart

Dare the unpastur'd dragon in his den?

Defenceless as thou wert, oh, where was then

Wisdom the mirror'd shield, or scorn the spear?

Or hadst thou waited the full cycle, when

Thy spirit should have fill'd its crescent sphere,

The monsters of life's waste had fled from thee like deer.

XXVIII

"The herded wolves, bold only to pursue;

The obscene ravens, clamorous o'er the dead;

The vultures to the conqueror's banner true

Who feed where Desolation first has fed,

And whose wings rain contagion; how they fled,

When, like Apollo, from his golden bow

The Pythian of the age one arrow sped

And smil'd! The spoilers tempt no second blow,

They fawn on the proud feet that spurn them lying low.

XXIX

"The sun comes forth, and many reptiles spawn;

He sets, and each ephemeral insect then

Is gather'd into death without a dawn,

And the immortal stars awake again;

So is it in the world of living men:

A godlike mind soars forth, in its delight

Making earth bare and veiling heaven, and when

It sinks, the swarms that dimm'd or shar'd its light

Leave to its kindred lamps the spirit's awful night."

XXX

Thus ceas'd she: and the mountain shepherds came,

Their garlands sere, their magic mantles rent;

The Pilgrim of Eternity, whose fame

Over his living head like Heaven is bent,

An early but enduring monument,

Came, veiling all the lightnings of his song

In sorrow; from her wilds Ierne sent

The sweetest lyrist of her saddest wrong,

And Love taught Grief to fall like music from his tongue.

XXXI

Midst others of less note, came one frail Form,

A phantom among men; companionless

As the last cloud of an expiring storm

Whose thunder is its knell; he, as I guess,

Had gaz'd on Nature's naked loveliness,

Actaeon-like, and now he fled astray

With feeble steps o'er the world's wilderness,

And his own thoughts, along that rugged way,

Pursu'd, like raging hounds, their father and their prey.

XXXII

A pardlike Spirit beautiful and swift—

A Love in desolation mask'd—a Power

Girt round with weakness—it can scarce uplift

The weight of the superincumbent hour;

It is a dying lamp, a falling shower,

A breaking billow; even whilst we speak

Is it not broken? On the withering flower

The killing sun smiles brightly: on a cheek

The life can burn in blood, even while the heart may break.

XXXIII

His head was bound with pansies overblown,

And faded violets, white, and pied, and blue;

And a light spear topp'd with a cypress cone,

Round whose rude shaft dark ivy-tresses grew

Yet dripping with the forest's noonday dew,

Vibrated, as the ever-beating heart

Shook the weak hand that grasp'd it; of that crew

He came the last, neglected and apart;

A herd-abandon'd deer struck by the hunter's dart.

XXXIV

All stood aloof, and at his partial moan

Smil'd through their tears; well knew that gentle band

Who in another's fate now wept his own,

As in the accents of an unknown land

He sung new sorrow; sad Urania scann'd

The Stranger's mien, and murmur'd: "Who art thou?"

He answer'd not, but with a sudden hand

Made bare his branded and ensanguin'd brow,

Which was like Cain's or Christ's—oh! that it should be so!

XXXV

What softer voice is hush'd over the dead?

Athwart what brow is that dark mantle thrown?

What form leans sadly o'er the white death-bed,

In mockery of monumental stone,

The heavy heart heaving without a moan?

If it be He, who, gentlest of the wise,

Taught, sooth'd, lov'd, honour'd the departed one,

Let me not vex, with inharmonious sighs,

The silence of that heart's accepted sacrifice.

XXXVI

Our Adonais has drunk poison—oh!

What deaf and viperous murderer could crown

Life's early cup with such a draught of woe?

The nameless worm would now itself disown:

It felt, yet could escape, the magic tone

Whose prelude held all envy, hate and wrong,

But what was howling in one breast alone,

Silent with expectation of the song,

Whose master's hand is cold, whose silver lyre unstrung.

XXXVII

Live thou, whose infamy is not thy fame!

Live! fear no heavier chastisement from me,

Thou noteless blot on a remember'd name!

But be thyself, and know thyself to be!

And ever at thy season be thou free

To spill the venom when thy fangs o'erflow;

Remorse and Self-contempt shall cling to thee;

Hot Shame shall burn upon thy secret brow,

And like a beaten hound tremble thou shalt—as now.

XXXVIII

Nor let us weep that our delight is fled

Far from these carrion kites that scream below;

He wakes or sleeps with the enduring dead;

Thou canst not soar where he is sitting now.

Dust to the dust! but the pure spirit shall flow

Back to the burning fountain whence it came,

A portion of the Eternal, which must glow

Through time and change, unquenchably the same,

Whilst thy cold embers choke the sordid hearth of shame.

XXXIX

Peace, peace! he is not dead, he doth not sleep,

He hath awaken'd from the dream of life;

'Tis we, who lost in stormy visions, keep

With phantoms an unprofitable strife,

And in mad trance, strike with our spirit's knife

Invulnerable nothings. *We* decay

Like corpses in a charnel; fear and grief

Convulse us and consume us day by day,

And cold hopes swarm like worms within our living clay.

XL

He has outsoar'd the shadow of our night;

Envy and calumny and hate and pain,

And that unrest which men miscall delight,

Can touch him not and torture not again;

From the contagion of the world's slow stain

He is secure, and now can never mourn

A heart grown cold, a head grown gray in vain;

Nor, when the spirit's self has ceas'd to burn,

With sparkless ashes load an unlamented urn.

XLI

He lives, he wakes—'tis Death is dead, not he;

Mourn not for Adonais. Thou young Dawn,

Turn all thy dew to splendour, for from thee

The spirit thou lamentest is not gone;

Ye caverns and ye forests, cease to moan!

Cease, ye faint flowers and fountains, and thou Air,

Which like a mourning veil thy scarf hadst thrown

O'er the abandon'd Earth, now leave it bare

Even to the joyous stars which smile on its despair!

XLII

He is made one with Nature: there is heard

His voice in all her music, from the moan

Of thunder, to the song of night's sweet bird;

He is a presence to be felt and known

In darkness and in light, from herb and stone,

Spreading itself where'er that Power may move

Which has withdrawn his being to its own;

Which wields the world with never-wearied love,

Sustains it from beneath, and kindles it above.

XLIII

He is a portion of the loveliness

Which once he made more lovely: he doth bear

His part, while the one Spirit's plastic stress

Sweeps through the dull dense world, compelling there

All new successions to the forms they wear;

Torturing th' unwilling dross that checks its flight

To its own likeness, as each mass may bear;

And bursting in its beauty and its might

From trees and beasts and men into the Heaven's light.

XLIV

The splendours of the firmament of time

May be eclips'd, but are extinguish'd not;

Like stars to their appointed height they climb,

And death is a low mist which cannot blot

The brightness it may veil. When lofty thought

Lifts a young heart above its mortal lair,

And love and life contend in it for what

Shall be its earthly doom, the dead live there

And move like winds of light on dark and stormy air.

XLV

    The inheritors of unfulfill'd renown

    Rose from their thrones, built beyond mortal thought,

    Far in the Unapparent. Chatterton

    Rose pale, his solemn agony had not

    Yet faded from him; Sidney, as he fought

    And as he fell and as he liv'd and lov'd

    Sublimely mild, a Spirit without spot,

    Arose; and Lucan, by his death approv'd:

Oblivion as they rose shrank like a thing reprov'd.

XLVI

    And many more, whose names on Earth are dark,

    But whose transmitted effluence cannot die

    So long as fire outlives the parent spark,

    Rose, rob'd in dazzling immortality.

    "Thou art become as one of us," they cry,

    "It was for thee yon kingless sphere has long

    Swung blind in unascended majesty,

    Silent alone amid a Heaven of Song.

Assume thy winged throne, thou Vesper of our throng!"

XLVII

    Who mourns for Adonais? Oh, come forth,

    Fond wretch! and know thyself and him aright.

Clasp with thy panting soul the pendulous Earth;

As from a centre, dart thy spirit's light

Beyond all worlds, until its spacious might

Satiate the void circumference: then shrink

Even to a point within our day and night;

And keep thy heart light lest it make thee sink

When hope has kindled hope, and lur'd thee to the brink.

XLVIII

Or go to Rome, which is the sepulchre,

Oh, not of him, but of our joy: 'tis nought

That ages, empires and religions there

Lie buried in the ravage they have wrought;

For such as he can lend—they borrow not

Glory from those who made the world their prey;

And he is gather'd to the kings of thought

Who wag'd contention with their time's decay,

And of the past are all that cannot pass away.

XLIX

Go thou to Rome—at once the Paradise,

The grave, the city, and the wilderness;

And where its wrecks like shatter'd mountains rise,

And flowering weeds, and fragrant copses dress

The bones of Desolation's nakedness

Pass, till the spirit of the spot shall lead

Thy footsteps to a slope of green access

Where, like an infant's smile, over the dead

A light of laughing flowers along the grass is spread;

L

And gray walls moulder round, on which dull Time

Feeds, like slow fire upon a hoary brand;

And one keen pyramid with wedge sublime,

Pavilioning the dust of him who plann'd

This refuge for his memory, doth stand

Like flame transform'd to marble; and beneath,

A field is spread, on which a newer band

Have pitch'd in Heaven's smile their camp of death,

Welcoming him we lose with scarce extinguish'd breath.

LI

Here pause: these graves are all too young as yet

To have outgrown the sorrow which consign'd

Its charge to each; and if the seal is set,

Here, on one fountain of a mourning mind,

Break it not thou! too surely shalt thou find

Thine own well full, if thou returnest home,

Of tears and gall. From the world's bitter wind

Seek shelter in the shadow of the tomb.

What Adonais is, why fear we to become?

LII

The One remains, the many change and pass;

Heaven's light forever shines, Earth's shadows fly;

Life, like a dome of many-colour'd glass,

Stains the white radiance of Eternity,

Until Death tramples it to fragments.—Die,

If thou wouldst be with that which thou dost seek!

Follow where all is fled!—Rome's azure sky,

Flowers, ruins, statues, music, words, are weak

The glory they transfuse with fitting truth to speak.

LIII

Why linger, why turn back, why shrink, my Heart?

Thy hopes are gone before: from all things here

They have departed; thou shouldst now depart!

A light is pass'd from the revolving year,

And man, and woman; and what still is dear

Attracts to crush, repels to make thee wither.

The soft sky smiles, the low wind whispers near:

'Tis Adonais calls! oh, hasten thither,

No more let Life divide what Death can join together.

LIV

That Light whose smile kindles the Universe,

That Beauty in which all things work and move,

That Benediction which the eclipsing Curse

Of birth can quench not, that sustaining Love

Which through the web of being blindly wove

By man and beast and earth and air and sea,

33

Burns bright or dim, as each are mirrors of

The fire for which all thirst; now beams on me,

Consuming the last clouds of cold mortality.

LV

The breath whose might I have invok'd in song

Descends on me; my spirit's bark is driven,

Far from the shore, far from the trembling throng

Whose sails were never to the tempest given;

The massy earth and sphered skies are riven!

I am borne darkly, fearfully, afar;

Whilst, burning through the inmost veil of Heaven,

The soul of Adonais, like a star,

Beacons from the abode where the Eternal are.

Love's Philosophy

The fountains mingle with the river
  And the rivers with the ocean,
The winds of heaven mix for ever
  With a sweet emotion;
Nothing in the world is single;
  All things by a law divine
In one spirit meet and mingle.
  Why not I with thine?—

See the mountains kiss high heaven
  And the waves clasp one another;
No sister-flower would be forgiven
  If it disdained its brother;
And the sunlight clasps the earth
  And the moonbeams kiss the sea:
What is all this sweet work worth
  If thou kiss not me?

The Triumph of Life

Swift as a spirit hastening to his task

Of glory & of good, the Sun sprang forth

Rejoicing in his splendour, & the mask

Of darkness fell from the awakened Earth.

The smokeless altars of the mountain snows

Flamed above crimson clouds, & at the birth

Of light, the Ocean's orison arose

To which the birds tempered their matin lay,

All flowers in field or forest which unclose

Their trembling eyelids to the kiss of day,

Swinging their censers in the element,

With orient incense lit by the new ray

Burned slow & inconsumably, & sent

Their odorous sighs up to the smiling air,

And in succession due, did Continent,

Isle, Ocean, & all things that in them wear

The form & character of mortal mould

Rise as the Sun their father rose, to bear

Their portion of the toil which he of old

Took as his own & then imposed on them;

But I, whom thoughts which must remain untold

Had kept as wakeful as the stars that gem

The cone of night, now they were laid asleep,

Stretched my faint limbs beneath the hoary stem

Which an old chestnut flung athwart the steep

Of a green Apennine: before me fled

The night; behind me rose the day; the Deep

Was at my feet, & Heaven above my head

When a strange trance over my fancy grew

Which was not slumber, for the shade it spread

Was so transparent that the scene came through

As clear as when a veil of light is drawn

O'er evening hills they glimmer; and I knew

That I had felt the freshness of that dawn,

Bathed in the same cold dew my brow & hair

And sate as thus upon that slope of lawn

Under the self same bough, & heard as there

The birds, the fountains & the Ocean hold

Sweet talk in music through the enamoured air.

And then a Vision on my brain was rolled.

As in that trance of wondrous thought I lay

This was the tenour of my waking dream.

Methought I sate beside a public way

Thick strewn with summer dust, & a great stream

Of people there was hurrying to & fro

Numerous as gnats upon the evening gleam,

All hastening onward, yet none seemed to know

Whither he went, or whence he came, or why

He made one of the multitude, yet so

Was borne amid the crowd as through the sky

One of the million leaves of summer's bier.—

Old age & youth, manhood & infancy,

Mixed in one mighty torrent did appear,

Some flying from the thing they feared & some

Seeking the object of another's fear,

And others as with steps towards the tomb

Pored on the trodden worms that crawled beneath,

And others mournfully within the gloom

Of their own shadow walked, and called it death ...

And some fled from it as it were a ghost,

Half fainting in the affliction of vain breath.

But more with motions which each other crost

Pursued or shunned the shadows the clouds threw

Or birds within the noonday ether lost,

Upon that path where flowers never grew;

And weary with vain toil & faint for thirst

Heard not the fountains whose melodious dew

Out of their mossy cells forever burst

Nor felt the breeze which from the forest told

Of grassy paths, & wood lawns interspersed

With overarching elms & caverns cold,

And violet banks where sweet dreams brood, but they

Pursued their serious folly as of old ....

And as I gazed methought that in the way

The throng grew wilder, as the woods of June

When the South wind shakes the extinguished day.—

And a cold glare, intenser than the noon

But icy cold, obscured with [[blank]] light

The Sun as he the stars. Like the young moon

When on the sunlit limits of the night

Her white shell trembles amid crimson air

And whilst the sleeping tempest gathers might

Doth, as a herald of its coming, bear

The ghost of her dead Mother, whose dim form

Bends in dark ether from her infant's chair,

So came a chariot on the silent storm

Of its own rushing splendour, and a Shape

So sate within as one whom years deform

Beneath a dusky hood & double cape

Crouching within the shadow of a tomb,

And o'er what seemed the head, a cloud like crape,

Was bent a dun & faint etherial gloom

Tempering the light; upon the chariot's beam

A Janus-visaged Shadow did assume

The guidance of that wonder-winged team.

The Shapes which drew it in thick lightnings

Were lost: I heard alone on the air's soft stream

The music of their ever moving wings.

All the four faces of that charioteer

Had their eyes banded . . . little profit brings

Speed in the van & blindness in the rear,

Nor then avail the beams that quench the Sun

Or that his banded eyes could pierce the sphere

Of all that is, has been, or will be done.—

So ill was the car guided, but it past

With solemn speed majestically on . . .

The crowd gave way, & I arose aghast,

Or seemed to rise, so mighty was the trance,

And saw like clouds upon the thunder blast

The million with fierce song and maniac dance

Raging around; such seemed the jubilee

As when to greet some conqueror's advance

Imperial Rome poured forth her living sea

From senatehouse & prison & theatre

When Freedom left those who upon the free

Had bound a yoke which soon they stooped to bear.

Nor wanted here the true similitude

Of a triumphal pageant, for where'er

The chariot rolled a captive multitude

Was driven; althose who had grown old in power

Or misery,—all who have their age subdued,

By action or by suffering, and whose hour

Was drained to its last sand in weal or woe,

So that the trunk survived both fruit & flower;

All those whose fame or infamy must grow

Till the great winter lay the form & name

Of their own earth with them forever low,

All but the sacred few who could not tame

Their spirits to the Conqueror, but as soon

As they had touched the world with living flame

Fled back like eagles to their native noon,

Of those who put aside the diadem

Of earthly thrones or gems, till the last one

Were there;—for they of Athens & Jerusalem

Were neither mid the mighty captives seen

Nor mid the ribald crowd that followed them

Or fled before .. Now swift, fierce & obscene

The wild dance maddens in the van, & those

Who lead it, fleet as shadows on the green,

Outspeed the chariot & without repose

Mix with each other in tempestuous measure

To savage music .... Wilder as it grows,

They, tortured by the agonizing pleasure,

Convulsed & on the rapid whirlwinds spun

Of that fierce spirit, whose unholy leisure

Was soothed by mischief since the world begun,

Throw back their heads & loose their streaming hair,

And in their dance round her who dims the Sun

Maidens & youths fling their wild arms in air

As their feet twinkle; they recede, and now

Bending within each other's atmosphere

Kindle invisibly; and as they glow

Like moths by light attracted & repelled,

Oft to new bright destruction come & go.

Till like two clouds into one vale impelled

That shake the mountains when their lightnings mingle

And die in rain,—the fiery band which held

Their natures, snaps . . . ere the shock cease to tingle

One falls and then another in the path

Senseless, nor is the desolation single,

Yet ere I can say *where* the chariot hath

Past over them; nor other trace I find

But as of foam after the Ocean's wrath

Is spent upon the desert shore.—Behind,

Old men, and women foully disarrayed

Shake their grey hair in the insulting wind,

Limp in the dance & strain, with limbs decayed,

Seeking to reach the light which leaves them still

Farther behind & deeper in the shade.

But not the less with impotence of will

They wheel, though ghastly shadows interpose

Round them & round each other, and fulfill

Their work and to the dust whence they arose

Sink & corruption veils them as they lie

And frost in these performs what fire in those.

Struck to the heart by this sad pageantry,

Half to myself I said, "And what is this?

Whose shape is that within the car? & why"-

I would have added—"is all here amiss?"

But a voice answered . . "Life" . . . I turned & knew

(O Heaven have mercy on such wretchedness!)

That what I thought was an old root which grew

To strange distortion out of the hill side

Was indeed one of that deluded crew,

And that the grass which methought hung so wide

And white, was but his thin discoloured hair,

And that the holes it vainly sought to hide

Were or had been eyes.—"If thou canst forbear

To join the dance, which I had well forborne,"

Said the grim Feature, of my thought aware,

"I will now tell that which to this deep scorn

Led me & my companions, and relate

The progress of the pageant since the morn;

"If thirst of knowledge doth not thus abate,

Follow it even to the night, but I

Am weary" . . . Then like one who with the weight

Of his own words is staggered, wearily

He paused, and ere he could resume, I cried,

"First who art thou?" . . . "Before thy memory

"I feared, loved, hated, suffered, did, & died,

And if the spark with which Heaven lit my spirit

Earth had with purer nutriment supplied

"Corruption would not now thus much inherit

Of what was once Rousseau—nor this disguise

Stained that within which still disdains to wear it.—

"If I have been extinguished, yet there rise

A thousand beacons from the spark I bore."—

"And who are those chained to the car?" "The Wise,

"The great, the unforgotten: they who wore

Mitres & helms & crowns, or wreathes of light,

Signs of thought's empire over thought; their lore

"Taught them not this—to know themselves; their might

Could not repress the mutiny within,

And for the morn of truth they feigned, deep night

"Caught them ere evening." "Who is he with chin

Upon his breast and hands crost on his chain?"

"The Child of a fierce hour; he sought to win

"The world, and lost all it did contain

Of greatness, in its hope destroyed; & more

Of fame & peace than Virtue's self can gain

"Without the opportunity which bore

Him on its eagle's pinion to the peak

From which a thousand climbers have before

"Fall'n as Napoleon fell."—I felt my cheek

Alter to see the great form pass away

Whose grasp had left the giant world so weak

That every pigmy kicked it as it lay—

And much I grieved to think how power & will

In opposition rule our mortal day—

And why God made irreconcilable

Good & the means of good; and for despair

I half disdained mine eye's desire to fill

With the spent vision of the times that were

And scarce have ceased to be . . . "Dost thou behold,"

Said then my guide, "those spoilers spoiled, Voltaire,

"Frederic, & Kant, Catherine, & Leopold,

Chained hoary anarch, demagogue & sage

Whose name the fresh world thinks already old—

"For in the battle Life & they did wage

She remained conqueror—I was overcome

By my own heart alone, which neither age

"Nor tears nor infamy nor now the tomb

Could temper to its object."—"Let them pass"—

I cried—"the world & its mysterious doom

"Is not so much more glorious than it was

That I desire to worship those who drew

New figures on its false & fragile glass

"As the old faded."—"Figures ever new

Rise on the bubble, paint them how you may;

We have but thrown, as those before us threw,

"Our shadows on it as it past away.

But mark, how chained to the triumphal chair

The mighty phantoms of an elder day—

"All that is mortal of great Plato there

Expiates the joy & woe his master knew not;

That star that ruled his doom was far too fair—

"And Life, where long that flower of Heaven grew not,

Conquered the heart by love which gold or pain

Or age or sloth or slavery could subdue not—

"And near [[blank]] walk the [[blank]] twain,

The tutor & his pupil, whom Dominion

Followed as tame as vulture in a chain.—

"The world was darkened beneath either pinion

Of him whom from the flock of conquerors

Fame singled as her thunderbearing minion;

"The other long outlived both woes & wars,

Throned in new thoughts of men, and still had kept

The jealous keys of truth's eternal doors

"If Bacon's spirit [[blank]] had not leapt

Like lightning out of darkness; he compelled

The Proteus shape of Nature's as it slept

"To wake & to unbar the caves that held

The treasure of the secrets of its reign—

See the great bards of old who inly quelled

"The passions which they sung, as by their strain

May well be known: their living melody

Tempers its own contagion to the vein

"Of those who are infected with it—I

Have suffered what I wrote, or viler pain!—

"And so my words were seeds of misery—

Even as the deeds of others."—"Not as theirs,"

I said—he pointed to a company

In which I recognized amid the heirs

Of Caesar's crime from him to Constantine,

The Anarchs old whose force & murderous snares

Had founded many a sceptre bearing line

And spread the plague of blood & gold abroad,

And Gregory & John and men divine

Who rose like shadows between Man & god

Till that eclipse, still hanging under Heaven,

Was worshipped by the world o'er which they strode

For the true Sun it quenched.—"Their power was given

But to destroy," replied the leader—"I

Am one of those who have created, even

"If it be but a world of agony."—

"Whence camest thou & whither goest thou?

How did thy course begin," I said, "& why?

"Mine eyes are sick of this perpetual flow

Of people, & my heart of one sad thought.—

Speak."—"Whence I came, partly I seem to know,

"And how & by what paths I have been brought

To this dread pass, methinks even thou mayst guess;

Why this should be my mind can compass not;

"Whither the conqueror hurries me still less.

But follow thou, & from spectator turn

Actor or victim in this wretchedness,

"And what thou wouldst be taught I then may learn

From thee.—Now listen . . . In the April prime

When all the forest tops began to burn

"With kindling green, touched by the azure clime

Of the young year, I found myself asleep

Under a mountain which from unknown time

"Had yawned into a cavern high & deep,

And from it came a gentle rivulet

Whose water like clear air in its calm sweep

"Bent the soft grass & kept for ever wet

The stems of the sweet flowers, and filled the grove

With sound which all who hear must needs forget

"All pleasure & all pain, all hate & love,

Which they had known before that hour of rest:

A sleeping mother then would dream not of

"The only child who died upon her breast

At eventide, a king would mourn no more

The crown of which his brow was dispossest

"When the sun lingered o'er the Ocean floor

To gild his rival's new prosperity.—

Thou wouldst forget thus vainly to deplore

"Ills, which if ills, can find no cure from thee,

The thought of which no other sleep will quell

Nor other music blot from memory—

"So sweet & deep is the oblivious spell.—

Whether my life had been before that sleep

The Heaven which I imagine, or a Hell

"Like this harsh world in which I wake to weep,

I know not. I arose & for a space

The scene of woods & waters seemed to keep,

"Though it was now broad day, a gentle trace

Of light diviner than the common Sun

Sheds on the common Earth, but all the place

"Was filled with many sounds woven into one

Oblivious melody, confusing sense

Amid the gliding waves & shadows dun;

"And as I looked the bright omnipresence

Of morning through the orient cavern flowed,

And the Sun's image radiantly intense

"Burned on the waters of the well that glowed

Like gold, and threaded all the forest maze

With winding paths of emerald fire—there stood

"Amid the sun, as he amid the blaze

Of his own glory, on the vibrating

Floor of the fountain, paved with flashing rays,

"A shape all light, which with one hand did fling

Dew on the earth, as if she were the Dawn

Whose invisible rain forever seemed to sing

"A silver music on the mossy lawn,

And still before her on the dusky grass

Iris her many coloured scarf had drawn.—

"In her right hand she bore a crystal glass

Mantling with bright Nepenthe;—the fierce splendour

Fell from her as she moved under the mass

"Of the deep cavern, & with palms so tender

Their tread broke not the mirror of its billow,

Glided along the river, and did bend her

"Head under the dark boughs, till like a willow

Her fair hair swept the bosom of the stream

That whispered with delight to be their pillow.—

"As one enamoured is upborne in dream

O'er lily-paven lakes mid silver mist

To wondrous music, so this shape might seem

"Partly to tread the waves with feet which kist

The dancing foam, partly to glide along

The airs that roughened the moist amethyst,

"Or the slant morning beams that fell among

The trees, or the soft shadows of the trees;

And her feet ever to the ceaseless song

"Of leaves & winds & waves & birds & bees

And falling drops moved in a measure new

Yet sweet, as on the summer evening breeze

"Up from the lake a shape of golden dew

Between two rocks, athwart the rising moon,

Moves up the east, where eagle never flew.—

"And still her feet, no less than the sweet tune

To which they moved, seemed as they moved, to blot

The thoughts of him who gazed on them, & soon

"All that was seemed as if it had been not,

As if the gazer's mind was strewn beneath

Her feet like embers, & she, thought by thought,

"Trampled its fires into the dust of death,

As Day upon the threshold of the east

Treads out the lamps of night, until the breath

"Of darkness reillumines even the least

Of heaven's living eyes—like day she came,

Making the night a dream; and ere she ceased

"To move, as one between desire and shame

Suspended, I said—'If, as it doth seem,

Thou comest from the realm without a name,

" 'Into this valley of perpetual dream,

Shew whence I came, and where I am, and why—

Pass not away upon the passing stream.'

" 'Arise and quench thy thirst,' was her reply,

And as a shut lily, stricken by the wand

Of dewy morning's vital alchemy,

"I rose; and, bending at her sweet command,

Touched with faint lips the cup she raised,

And suddenly my brain became as sand

"Where the first wave had more than half erased

The track of deer on desert Labrador,

Whilst the fierce wolf from which they fled amazed

"Leaves his stamp visibly upon the shore

Until the second bursts—so on my sight

Burst a new Vision never seen before.—

"And the fair shape waned in the coming light

As veil by veil the silent splendour drops

From Lucifer, amid the chrysolite

"Of sunrise ere it strike the mountain tops—

And as the presence of that fairest planet

Although unseen is felt by one who hopes

"That his day's path may end as he began it

In that star's smile, whose light is like the scent

Of a jonquil when evening breezes fan it,

"Or the soft note in which his dear lament

The Brescian shepherd breathes, or the caress

That turned his weary slumber to content.—

"So knew I in that light's severe excess

The presence of that shape which on the stream

Moved, as I moved along the wilderness,

"More dimly than a day appearing dream,

The ghost of a forgotten form of sleep

A light from Heaven whose half extinguished beam

"Through the sick day in which we wake to weep

Glimmers, forever sought, forever lost.—

So did that shape its obscure tenour keep

"Beside my path, as silent as a ghost;

But the new Vision, and its cold bright car,

With savage music, stunning music, crost

"The forest, and as if from some dread war

Triumphantly returning, the loud million

Fiercely extolled the fortune of her star.—

"A moving arch of victory the vermilion

And green & azure plumes of Iris had

Built high over her wind-winged pavilion,

"And underneath aetherial glory clad

The wilderness, and far before her flew

The tempest of the splendour which forbade

Shadow to fall from leaf or stone;—the crew

Seemed in that light like atomies that dance

Within a sunbeam.—Some upon the new

"Embroidery of flowers that did enhance

The grassy vesture of the desart, played,

Forgetful of the chariot's swift advance;

"Others stood gazing till within the shade

Of the great mountain its light left them dim.—

Others outspeeded it, and others made

"Circles around it like the clouds that swim

Round the high moon in a bright sea of air,

And more did follow, with exulting hymn,

52

"The chariot & the captives fettered there,

But all like bubbles on an eddying flood

Fell into the same track at last & were

"Borne onward.—I among the multitude

Was swept; me sweetest flowers delayed not long,

Me not the shadow nor the solitude,

"Me not the falling stream's Lethean song,

Me, not the phantom of that early form

Which moved upon its motion,—but among

"The thickest billows of the living storm

I plunged, and bared my bosom to the clime

Of that cold light, whose airs too soon deform.—

"Before the chariot had begun to climb

The opposing steep of that mysterious dell,

Behold a wonder worthy of the rhyme

"Of him whom from the lowest depths of Hell

Through every Paradise & through all glory

Love led serene, & who returned to tell

"In words of hate & awe the wondrous story

How all things are transfigured, except Love;

For deaf as is a sea which wrath makes hoary

"The world can hear not the sweet notes that move

The sphere whose light is melody to lovers—-

A wonder worthy of his rhyme—the grove

"Grew dense with shadows to its inmost covers,

The earth was grey with phantoms, & the air

Was peopled with dim forms, as when there hovers

"A flock of vampire-bats before the glare

Of the tropic sun, bring ere evening

Strange night upon some Indian isle,—thus were

"Phantoms diffused around, & some did fling

Shadows of shadows, yet unlike themselves,

Behind them, some like eaglets on the wing

"Were lost in the white blaze, others like elves

Danced in a thousand unimagined shapes

Upon the sunny streams & grassy shelves;

"And others sate chattering like restless apes

On vulgar paws and voluble like fire.

Some made a cradle of the ermined capes

"Of kingly mantles, some upon the tiar

Of pontiffs sate like vultures, others played

Within the crown which girt with empire

"A baby's or an idiot's brow, & made

Their nests in it; the old anatomies

Sate hatching their bare brood under the shade

"Of demon wings, and laughed from their dead eyes

To reassume the delegated power

Arrayed in which these worms did monarchize

"Who make this earth their charnel.—Others more

Humble, like falcons sate upon the fist

Of common men, and round their heads did soar,

"Or like small gnats & flies, as thick as mist

On evening marshes, thronged about the brow

Of lawyer, statesman, priest & theorist,

"And others like discoloured flakes of snow

On fairest bosoms & the sunniest hair

Fell, and were melted by the youthful glow

"Which they extinguished; for like tears, they were

A veil to those from whose faint lids they rained

In drops of sorrow.—I became aware

"Of whence those forms proceeded which thus stained

The track in which we moved; after brief space

From every form the beauty slowly waned,

"From every firmest limb & fairest face

The strength & freshness fell like dust, & left

The action & the shape without the grace

"Of life; the marble brow of youth was cleft

With care, and in the eyes where once hope shone

Desire like a lioness bereft

"Of its last cub, glared ere it died; each one

Of that great crowd sent forth incessantly

These shadows, numerous as the dead leaves blown

"In Autumn evening from a popular tree—

Each, like himself & like each other were,

At first, but soon distorted, seemed to be

"Obscure clouds moulded by the casual air;

And of this stuff the car's creative ray

Wrought all the busy phantoms that were there

"As the sun shapes the clouds—thus, on the way

Mask after mask fell from the countenance

And form of all, and long before the day

"Was old, the joy which waked like Heaven's glance

The sleepers in the oblivious valley, died,

And some grew weary of the ghastly dance

"And fell, as I have fallen by the way side,

Those soonest from whose forms most shadows past

And least of strength & beauty did abide."—

"Then, what is Life?" I said . . . the cripple cast

His eye upon the car which now had rolled

Onward, as if that look must be the last,

And answered .... "Happy those for whom the fold

Of ...

Alastor; or, The Spirit of Solitude

Nondum amabam, et amare amabam, quaerebam quid amarem, amans amare.—
Confess. St. August.

Earth, ocean, air, belovèd brotherhood!

If our great Mother has imbued my soul

With aught of natural piety to feel

Your love, and recompense the boon with mine;

If dewy morn, and odorous noon, and even,

With sunset and its gorgeous ministers,

And solemn midnight's tingling silentness;

If autumn's hollow sighs in the sere wood,

And winter robing with pure snow and crowns

Of starry ice the grey grass and bare boughs;

If spring's voluptuous pantings when she breathes

Her first sweet kisses, have been dear to me;

If no bright bird, insect, or gentle beast

I consciously have injured, but still loved

And cherished these my kindred; then forgive

This boast, belovèd brethren, and withdraw

No portion of your wonted favour now!

Mother of this unfathomable world!

Favour my solemn song, for I have loved

Thee ever, and thee only; I have watched

Thy shadow, and the darkness of thy steps,

And my heart ever gazes on the depth

Of thy deep mysteries. I have made my bed

In charnels and on coffins, where black death

Keeps record of the trophies won from thee,

Hoping to still these obstinate questionings

Of thee and thine, by forcing some lone ghost

Thy messenger, to render up the tale

Of what we are. In lone and silent hours,

When night makes a weird sound of its own stillness,

Like an inspired and desperate alchymist

Staking his very life on some dark hope,

Have I mixed awful talk and asking looks

With my most innocent love, until strange tears

Uniting with those breathless kisses, made

Such magic as compels the charmèd night

To render up thy charge:...and, though ne'er yet

Thou hast unveiled thy inmost sanctuary,

Enough from incommunicable dream,

And twilight phantasms, and deep noon-day thought,

Has shone within me, that serenely now

And moveless, as a long-forgotten lyre

Suspended in the solitary dome

Of some mysterious and deserted fane,

I wait thy breath, Great Parent, that my strain

May modulate with murmurs of the air,

And motions of the forests and the sea,

And voice of living beings, and woven hymns

Of night and day, and the deep heart of man.

There was a Poet whose untimely tomb
No human hands with pious reverence reared,
But the charmed eddies of autumnal winds
Built o'er his mouldering bones a pyramid
Of mouldering leaves in the waste wilderness:—
A lovely youth,—no mourning maiden decked
With weeping flowers, or votive cypress wreath,
The lone couch of his everlasting sleep:—
Gentle, and brave, and generous,—no lorn bard
Breathed o'er his dark fate one melodious sigh:
He lived, he died, he sung, in solitude.
Strangers have wept to hear his passionate notes,
And virgins, as unknown he passed, have pined
And wasted for fond love of his wild eyes.
The fire of those soft orbs has ceased to burn,
And Silence, too enamoured of that voice,
Locks its mute music in her rugged cell.

By solemn vision, and bright silver dream,
His infancy was nurtured. Every sight
And sound from the vast earth and ambient air,
Sent to his heart its choicest impulses.
The fountains of divine philosophy
Fled not his thirsting lips, and all of great,
Or good, or lovely, which the sacred past

In truth or fable consecrates, he felt

And knew. When early youth had past, he left

His cold fireside and alienated home

To seek strange truths in undiscovered lands.

Many a wide waste and tangled wilderness

Has lured his fearless steps; and he has bought

With his sweet voice and eyes, from savage men,

His rest and food. Nature's most secret steps

He like her shadow has pursued, where'er

The red volcano overcanopies

Its fields of snow and pinnacles of ice

With burning smoke, or where bitumen lakes

On black bare pointed islets ever beat

With sluggish surge, or where the secret caves

Rugged and dark, winding among the springs

Of fire and poison, inaccessible

To avarice or pride, their starry domes

Of diamond and of gold expand above

Numberless and immeasurable halls,

Frequent with crystal column, and clear shrines

Of pearl, and thrones radiant with chrysolite.

Nor had that scene of ampler majesty

Than gems or gold, the varying roof of heaven

And the green earth lost in his heart its claims

To love and wonder; he would linger long

In lonesome vales, making the wild his home,

Until the doves and squirrels would partake

From his innocuous hand his bloodless food,

Lured by the gentle meaning of his looks,

And the wild antelope, that starts whene'er

The dry leaf rustles in the brake, suspend

Her timid steps to gaze upon a form

More graceful than her own.

                    His wandering step

Obedient to high thoughts, has visited

The awful ruins of the days of old:

Athens, and Tyre, and Balbec, and the waste

Where stood Jerusalem, the fallen towers

Of Babylon, the eternal pyramids,

Memphis and Thebes, and whatsoe'er of strange

Sculptured on alabaster obelisk,

Or jasper tomb, or mutilated sphynx,

Dark Æthiopia in her desert hills

Conceals. Among the ruined temples there,

Stupendous columns, and wild images

Of more than man, where marble daemons watch

The Zodiac's brazen mystery, and dead men

Hang their mute thoughts on the mute walls around,

He lingered, poring on memorials

Of the world's youth, through the long burning day

Gazed on those speechless shapes, nor, when the moon

Filled the mysterious halls with floating shades

Suspended he that task, but ever gazed

And gazed, till meaning on his vacant mind
Flashed like strong inspiration, and he saw
The thrilling secrets of the birth of time.

Meanwhile an Arab maiden brought his food,
Her daily portion, from her father's tent,
And spread her matting for his couch, and stole
From duties and repose to tend his steps:—
Enamoured, yet not daring for deep awe
To speak her love:—and watched his nightly sleep,
Sleepless herself, to gaze upon his lips
Parted in slumber, whence the regular breath
Of innocent dreams arose: then, when red morn
Made paler the pale moon, to her cold home
Wildered, and wan, and panting, she returned.

The Poet wandering on, through Arabie
And Persia, and the wild Carmanian waste,
And o'er the aërial mountains which pour down
Indus and Oxus from their icy caves,
In joy and exultation held his way;
Till in the vale of Cashmire, far within
Its loneliest dell, where odorous plants entwine
Beneath the hollow rocks a natural bower,
Beside a sparkling rivulet he stretched
His languid limbs. A vision on his sleep
There came, a dream of hopes that never yet

Had flushed his cheek. He dreamed a veilèd maid

Sate near him, talking in low solemn tones.

Her voice was like the voice of his own soul

Heard in the calm of thought; its music long,

Like woven sounds of streams and breezes, held

His inmost sense suspended in its web

Of many-coloured woof and shifting hues.

Knowledge and truth and virtue were her theme,

And lofty hopes of divine liberty,

Thoughts the most dear to him, and poesy,

Herself a poet. Soon the solemn mood

Of her pure mind kindled through all her frame

A permeating fire: wild numbers then

She raised, with voice stifled in tremulous sobs

Subdued by its own pathos: her fair hands

Were bare alone, sweeping from some strange harp

Strange symphony, and in their branching veins

The eloquent blood told an ineffable tale.

The beating of her heart was heard to fill

The pauses of her music, and her breath

Tumultuously accorded with those fits

Of intermitted song. Sudden she rose,

As if her heart impatiently endured

Its bursting burthen: at the sound he turned,

And saw by the warm light of their own life

Her glowing limbs beneath the sinuous veil

Of woven wind, her outspread arms now bare,

Her dark locks floating in the breath of night,

Her beamy bending eyes, her parted lips

Outstretched, and pale, and quivering eagerly.

His strong heart sunk and sickened with excess

Of love. He reared his shuddering limbs and quelled

His gasping breath, and spread his arms to meet

Her panting bosom:...she drew back a while,

Then, yielding to the irresistible joy,

With frantic gesture and short breathless cry

Folded his frame in her dissolving arms.

Now blackness veiled his dizzy eyes, and night

Involved and swallowed up the vision; sleep,

Like a dark flood suspended in its course

Rolled back its impulse on his vacant brain.

      Roused by the shock he started from his trance—

The cold white light of morning, the blue moon

Low in the west, the clear and garish hills,

The distinct valley and the vacant woods,

Spread round him where he stood. Whither have fled

The hues of heaven that canopied his bower

Of yesternight? The sounds that soothed his sleep,

The mystery and the majesty of Earth,

The joy, the exultation? His wan eyes

Gaze on the empty scene as vacantly

As ocean's moon looks on the moon in heaven.

The spirit of sweet human love has sent

A vision to the sleep of him who spurned

Her choicest gifts. He eagerly pursues

Beyond the realms of dream that fleeting shade;

He overleaps the bounds. Alas! Alas!

Were limbs and breath and being intertwined

Thus treacherously? Lost, lost, for ever lost,

In the wide pathless desert of dim sleep,

That beautiful shape! Does the dark gate of death

Conduct to thy mysterious paradise,

O Sleep? Does the bright arch of rainbow clouds,

And pendent mountains seen in the calm lake,

Lead only to a black and watery depth,

While death's blue vault, with loathliest vapours hung,

Where every shade which the foul grave exhales

Hides its dead eye from the detested day,

Conduct, O Sleep, to thy delightful realms?

This doubt with sudden tide flowed on his heart,

The insatiate hope which it awakened stung

His brain even like despair.

                While daylight held

The sky, the Poet kept mute conference

With his still soul. At night the passion came,

Like the fierce fiend of a distempered dream,

And shook him from his rest, and led him forth

Into the darkness.—As an eagle grasped

In folds of the green serpent, feels her breast

Burn with the poison, and precipitates

Through night and day, tempest, and calm, and cloud,

Frantic with dizzying anguish, her blind flight

O'er the wide aëry wilderness: thus driven

By the bright shadow of that lovely dream,

Beneath the cold glare of the desolate night,

Through tangled swamps and deep precipitous dells,

Startling with careless step the moonlight snake,

He fled. Red morning dawned upon his flight,

Shedding the mockery of its vital hues

Upon his cheek of death. He wandered on

Till vast Aornos, seen from Petra's steep,

Hung o'er the low horizon like a cloud;

Through Balk, and where the desolated tombs

Of Parthian kings scatter to every wind

Their wasting dust, wildly he wandered on,

Day after day a weary waste of hours,

Bearing within his life the brooding care

That ever fed on its decaying flame.

And now his limbs were lean; his scattered hair

Sered by the autumn of strange suffering

Sung dirges in the wind; his listless hand

Hung like dead bone within its withered skin;

Life, and the lustre that consumed it, shone

As in a furnace burning secretly

From his dark eyes alone. The cottagers,

Who ministered with human charity

His human wants, beheld with wondering awe
Their fleeting visitant. The mountaineer,
Encountering on some dizzy precipice
That spectral form, deemed that the Spirit of wind
With lightning eyes, and eager breath, and feet
Disturbing not the drifted snow, had paused
In its career: the infant would conceal
His troubled visage in his mother's robe
In terror at the glare of those wild eyes,
To remember their strange light in many a dream
Of after-times; but youthful maidens, taught
By nature, would interpret half the woe
That wasted him, would call him with false names
Brother, and friend, would press his pallid hand
At parting, and watch, dim through tears, the path
Of his departure from their father's door.

     At length upon the lone Chorasmian shore
He paused, a wide and melancholy waste
Of putrid marshes. A strong impulse urged
His steps to the sea-shore. A swan was there,
Beside a sluggish stream among the reeds.
It rose as he approached, and with strong wings
Scaling the upward sky, bent its bright course
High over the immeasurable main.
His eyes pursued its flight.—"Thou hast a home,
Beautiful bird; thou voyagest to thine home,

Where thy sweet mate will twine her downy neck

With thine, and welcome thy return with eyes

Bright in the lustre of their own fond joy.

And what am I that I should linger here,

With voice far sweeter than thy dying notes,

Spirit more vast than thine, frame more attuned

To beauty, wasting these surpassing powers

In the deaf air, to the blind earth, and heaven

That echoes not my thoughts?" A gloomy smile

Of desperate hope wrinkled his quivering lips.

For sleep, he knew, kept most relentlessly

Its precious charge, and silent death exposed,

Faithless perhaps as sleep, a shadowy lure,

With doubtful smile mocking its own strange charms.

      Startled by his own thoughts he looked around.

There was no fair fiend near him, not a sight

Or sound of awe but in his own deep mind.

A little shallop floating near the shore

Caught the impatient wandering of his gaze.

It had been long abandoned, for its sides

Gaped wide with many a rift, and its frail joints

Swayed with the undulations of the tide.

A restless impulse urged him to embark

And meet lone Death on the drear ocean's waste;

For well he knew that mighty Shadow loves

The slimy caverns of the populous deep.

The day was fair and sunny: sea and sky

Drank its inspiring radiance, and the wind

Swept strongly from the shore, blackening the waves.

Following his eager soul, the wanderer

Leaped in the boat, he spread his cloak aloft

On the bare mast, and took his lonely seat,

And felt the boat speed o'er the tranquil sea

Like a torn cloud before the hurricane.

As one that in a silver vision floats

Obedient to the sweep of odorous winds

Upon resplendent clouds, so rapidly

Along the dark and ruffled waters fled

The straining boat.—A whirlwind swept it on,

With fierce gusts and precipitating force,

Through the white ridges of the chafèd sea.

The waves arose. Higher and higher still

Their fierce necks writhed beneath the tempest's scourge

Like serpents struggling in a vulture's grasp.

Calm and rejoicing in the fearful war

Of wave ruining on wave, and blast on blast

Descending, and black flood on whirlpool driven

With dark obliterating course, he sate:

As if their genii were the ministers

Appointed to conduct him to the light

Of those belovèd eyes, the Poet sate

Holding the steady helm. Evening came on,

The beams of sunset hung their rainbow hues

High 'mid the shifting domes of sheeted spray

That canopied his path o'er the waste deep;

Twilight, ascending slowly from the east,

Entwined in duskier wreaths her braided locks

O'er the fair front and radiant eyes of day;

Night followed, clad with stars. On every side

More horribly the multitudinous streams

Of ocean's mountainous waste to mutual war

Rushed in dark tumult thundering, as to mock

The calm and spangled sky. The little boat

Still fled before the storm; still fled, like foam

Down the steep cataract of a wintry river;

Now pausing on the edge of the riven wave;

Now leaving far behind the bursting mass

That fell, convulsing ocean. Safely fled—

As if that frail and wasted human form,

Had been an elemental god.

            At midnight

The moon arose: and lo! the ethereal cliffs

Of Caucasus, whose icy summits shone

Among the stars like sunlight, and around

Whose caverned base the whirlpools and the waves

Bursting and eddying irresistibly

Rage and resound for ever.—Who shall save?—

The boat fled on,—the boiling torrent drove,—

The crags closed round with black and jaggèd arms,

The shattered mountain overhung the sea,

And faster still, beyond all human speed,

Suspended on the sweep of the smooth wave,

The little boat was driven. A cavern there

Yawned, and amid its slant and winding depths

Ingulfed the rushing sea. The boat fled on

With unrelaxing speed.—"Vision and Love!"

The Poet cried aloud, "I have beheld

The path of thy departure. Sleep and death

Shall not divide us long!"

                              The boat pursued

The windings of the cavern. Daylight shone

At length upon that gloomy river's flow;

Now, where the fiercest war among the waves

Is calm, on the unfathomable stream

The boat moved slowly. Where the mountain, riven,

Exposed those black depths to the azure sky,

Ere yet the flood's enormous volume fell

Even to the base of Caucasus, with sound

That shook the everlasting rocks, the mass

Filled with one whirlpool all that ample chasm;

Stair above stair the eddying waters rose,

Circling immeasurably fast, and laved

With alternating dash the gnarlèd roots

Of mighty trees, that stretched their giant arms

In darkness over it. I' the midst was left,

Reflecting, yet distorting every cloud,

A pool of treacherous and tremendous calm.

Seized by the sway of the ascending stream,

With dizzy swiftness, round, and round, and round,

Ridge after ridge the straining boat arose,

Till on the verge of the extremest curve,

Where, through an opening of the rocky bank,

The waters overflow, and a smooth spot

Of glassy quiet mid those battling tides

Is left, the boat paused shuddering.—Shall it sink

Down the abyss? Shall the reverting stress

Of that resistless gulf embosom it?

Now shall it fall?—A wandering stream of wind,

Breathed from the west, has caught the expanded sail,

And, lo! with gentle motion, between banks

Of mossy slope, and on a placid stream,

Beneath a woven grove it sails, and, hark!

The ghastly torrent mingles its far roar,

With the breeze murmuring in the musical woods.

Where the embowering trees recede, and leave

A little space of green expanse, the cove

Is closed by meeting banks, whose yellow flowers

For ever gaze on their own drooping eyes,

Reflected in the crystal calm. The wave

Of the boat's motion marred their pensive task,

Which nought but vagrant bird, or wanton wind,

Or falling spear-grass, or their own decay

Had e'er disturbed before. The Poet longed

To deck with their bright hues his withered hair,

But on his heart its solitude returned,

And he forbore. Not the strong impulse hid

In those flushed cheeks, bent eyes, and shadowy frame

Had yet performed its ministry: it hung

Upon his life, as lightning in a cloud

Gleams, hovering ere it vanish, ere the floods

Of night close over it.

                       The noonday sun

Now shone upon the forest, one vast mass

Of mingling shade, whose brown magnificence

A narrow vale embosoms. There, huge caves

Scooped in the dark base of their aëry rocks

Mocking its moans, respond and roar for ever.

The meeting boughs and implicated leaves

Wove twilight o'er the Poet's path, as led

By love, or dream, or god, or mightier Death,

He sought in Nature's dearest haunt, some bank

Her cradle, and his sepulchre. More dark

And dark the shades accumulate. The oak,

Expanding its immense and knotty arms,

Embraces the light beech. The pyramids

Of the tall cedar overarching, frame

Most solemn domes within, and far below,

Like clouds suspended in an emerald sky,

The ash and the acacia floating hang

Tremulous and pale. Like restless serpents, clothed

In rainbow and in fire, the parasites,

Starred with ten thousand blossoms, flow around

The grey trunks, and, as gamesome infants' eyes,

With gentle meanings, and most innocent wiles,

Fold their beams round the hearts of those that love,

These twine their tendrils with the wedded boughs

Uniting their close union; the woven leaves

Make net-work of the dark blue light of day,

And the night's noontide clearness, mutable

As shapes in the weird clouds. Soft mossy lawns

Beneath these canopies extend their swells,

Fragrant with perfumed herbs, and eyed with blooms

Minute yet beautiful. One darkest glen

Sends from its woods of musk-rose, twined with jasmine,

A soul-dissolving odour, to invite

To some more lovely mystery. Through the dell,

Silence and Twilight here, twin-sisters, keep

Their noonday watch, and sail among the shades,

Like vaporous shapes half seen; beyond, a well,

Dark, gleaming, and of most translucent wave,

Images all the woven boughs above,

And each depending leaf, and every speck

Of azure sky, darting between their chasms;

Nor aught else in the liquid mirror laves

Its portraiture, but some inconstant star

Between one foliaged lattice twinkling fair,

Or painted bird, sleeping beneath the moon,

Or gorgeous insect floating motionless,

Unconscious of the day, ere yet his wings

Have spread their glories to the gaze of noon.

Hither the Poet came. His eyes beheld

Their own wan light through the reflected lines

Of his thin hair, distinct in the dark depth

Of that still fountain; as the human heart,

Gazing in dreams over the gloomy grave,

Sees its own treacherous likeness there. He heard

The motion of the leaves, the grass that sprung

Startled and glanced and trembled even to feel

An unaccustomed presence, and the sound

Of the sweet brook that from the secret springs

Of that dark fountain rose. A Spirit seemed

To stand beside him—clothed in no bright robes

Of shadowy silver or enshrining light,

Borrowed from aught the visible world affords

Of grace, or majesty, or mystery;—

But, undulating woods, and silent well,

And leaping rivulet, and evening gloom

Now deepening the dark shades, for speech assuming,

Held commune with him, as if he and it

Were all that was,—only... when his regard

Was raised by intense pensiveness,... two eyes,

Two starry eyes, hung in the gloom of thought,

And seemed with their serene and azure smiles

To beckon him.

                       Obedient to the light

That shone within his soul, he went, pursuing

The windings of the dell.—The rivulet

Wanton and wild, through many a green ravine

Beneath the forest flowed. Sometimes it fell

Among the moss, with hollow harmony

Dark and profound. Now on the polished stones

It danced; like childhood laughing as it went:

Then, through the plain in tranquil wanderings crept,

Reflecting every herb and drooping bud

That overhung its quietness.—"O stream!

Whose source is inaccessibly profound,

Whither do thy mysterious waters tend?

Thou imagest my life. Thy darksome stillness,

Thy dazzling waves, thy loud and hollow gulfs,

Thy searchless fountain, and invisible course

Have each their type in me: and the wide sky,

And measureless ocean may declare as soon

What oozy cavern or what wandering cloud

Contains thy waters, as the universe

Tell where these living thoughts reside, when stretched

Upon thy flowers my bloodless limbs shall waste
I' the passing wind!"

                    Beside the grassy shore
Of the small stream he went; he did impress
On the green moss his tremulous step, that caught
Strong shuddering from his burning limbs. As one
Roused by some joyous madness from the couch
Of fever, he did move; yet, not like him,
Forgetful of the grave, where, when the flame
Of his frail exultation shall be spent,
He must descend. With rapid steps he went
Beneath the shade of trees, beside the flow
Of the wild babbling rivulet; and now
The forest's solemn canopies were changed
For the uniform and lightsome evening sky.
Grey rocks did peep from the spare moss, and stemmed
The struggling brook: tall spires of windlestrae
Threw their thin shadows down the rugged slope,
And nought but gnarlèd roots of ancient pines
Branchless and blasted, clenched with grasping roots
The unwilling soil. A gradual change was here,
Yet ghastly. For, as fast years flow away,
The smooth brow gathers, and the hair grows thin
And white, and where irradiate dewy eyes
Had shone, gleam stony orbs:—so from his steps
Bright flowers departed, and the beautiful shade

77

Of the green groves, with all their odorous winds

And musical motions. Calm, he still pursued

The stream, that with a larger volume now

Rolled through the labyrinthine dell; and there

Fretted a path through its descending curves

With its wintry speed. On every side now rose

Rocks, which, in unimaginable forms,

Lifted their black and barren pinnacles

In the light of evening, and its precipice

Obscuring the ravine, disclosed above,

Mid toppling stones, black gulfs and yawning caves,

Whose windings gave ten thousand various tongues

To the loud stream. Lo! where the pass expands

Its stony jaws, the abrupt mountain breaks,

And seems, with its accumulated crags,

To overhang the world: for wide expand

Beneath the wan stars and descending moon

Islanded seas, blue mountains, mighty streams,

Dim tracts and vast, robed in the lustrous gloom

Of leaden-coloured even, and fiery hills

Mingling their flames with twilight, on the verge

Of the remote horizon. The near scene,

In naked and severe simplicity,

Made contrast with the universe. A pine,

Rock-rooted, stretched athwart the vacancy

Its swinging boughs, to each inconstant blast

Yielding one only response, at each pause,

In most familiar cadence, with the howl

The thunder and the hiss of homeless streams

Mingling its solemn song, whilst the broad river,

Foaming and hurrying o'er its rugged path,

Fell into that immeasurable void,

Scattering its waters to the passing winds.

     Yet the grey precipice and solemn pine

And torrent, were not all;—one silent nook

Was there. Even on the edge of that vast mountain,

Upheld by knotty roots and fallen rocks,

It overlooked in its serenity

The dark earth, and the bending vault of stars.

It was a tranquil spot, that seemed to smile

Even in the lap of horror. Ivy clasped

The fissured stones with its entwining arms,

And did embower with leaves for ever green,

And berries dark, the smooth and even space

Of its inviolated floor, and here

The children of the autumnal whirlwind bore,

In wanton sport, those bright leaves, whose decay,

Red, yellow, or ethereally pale,

Rivals the pride of summer. 'Tis the haunt

Of every gentle wind, whose breath can teach

The wilds to love tranquillity. One step,

One human step alone, has ever broken

The stillness of its solitude:—one voice

Alone inspired its echoes;—even that voice

Which hither came, floating among the winds,

And led the loveliest among human forms

To make their wild haunts the depository

Of all the grace and beauty that endued

Its motions, render up its majesty,

Scatter its music on the unfeeling storm,

And to the damp leaves and blue cavern mould,

Nurses of rainbow flowers and branching moss,

Commit the colours of that varying cheek,

That snowy breast, those dark and drooping eyes.

    The dim and hornèd moon hung low, and poured

A sea of lustre on the horizon's verge

That overflowed its mountains. Yellow mist

Filled the unbounded atmosphere, and drank

Wan moonlight even to fulness: not a star

Shone, not a sound was heard; the very winds,

Danger's grim playmates, on that precipice

Slept, clasped in his embrace.—O, storm of death!

Whose sightless speed divides this sullen night:

And thou, colossal Skeleton, that, still

Guiding its irresistible career

In thy devastating omnipotence,

Art king of this frail world, from the red field

Of slaughter, from the reeking hospital,

The patriot's sacred couch, the snowy bed

Of innocence, the scaffold and the throne,

A mighty voice invokes thee. Ruin calls

His brother Death. A rare and regal prey

He hath prepared, prowling around the world;

Glutted with which thou mayst repose, and men

Go to their graves like flowers or creeping worms,

Nor ever more offer at thy dark shrine

The unheeded tribute of a broken heart.

When on the threshold of the green recess

The wanderer's footsteps fell, he knew that death

Was on him. Yet a little, ere it fled,

Did he resign his high and holy soul

To images of the majestic past,

That paused within his passive being now,

Like winds that bear sweet music, when they breathe

Through some dim latticed chamber. He did place

His pale lean hand upon the rugged trunk

Of the old pine. Upon an ivied stone

Reclined his languid head, his limbs did rest,

Diffused and motionless, on the smooth brink

Of that obscurest chasm;—and thus he lay,

Surrendering to their final impulses

The hovering powers of life. Hope and despair,

The torturers, slept; no mortal pain or fear

Marred his repose, the influxes of sense,

And his own being unalloyed by pain,

Yet feebler and more feeble, calmly fed

The stream of thought, till he lay breathing there

At peace, and faintly smiling:—his last sight

Was the great moon, which o'er the western line

Of the wide world her mighty horn suspended,

With whose dun beams inwoven darkness seemed

To mingle. Now upon the jaggèd hills

It rests, and still as the divided frame

Of the vast meteor sunk, the Poet's blood,

That ever beat in mystic sympathy

With nature's ebb and flow, grew feebler still:

And when two lessening points of light alone

Gleamed through the darkness, the alternate gasp

Of his faint respiration scarce did stir

The stagnate night:—till the minutest ray

Was quenched, the pulse yet lingered in his heart.

It paused—it fluttered. But when heaven remained

Utterly black, the murky shades involved

An image, silent, cold, and motionless,

As their own voiceless earth and vacant air.

Even as a vapour fed with golden beams

That ministered on sunlight, ere the west

Eclipses it, was now that wondrous frame—

No sense, no motion, no divinity—

A fragile lute, on whose harmonious strings

The breath of heaven did wander—a bright stream

Once fed with many-voicèd waves—a dream

Of youth, which night and time have quenched for ever,
Still, dark, and dry, and unremembered now.

    O, for Medea's wondrous alchemy,
Which wheresoe'er it fell made the earth gleam
With bright flowers, and the wintry boughs exhale
From vernal blooms fresh fragrance! O, that God,
Profuse of poisons, would concede the chalice
Which but one living man has drained, who now,
Vessel of deathless wrath, a slave that feels
No proud exemption in the blighting curse
He bears, over the world wanders for ever,
Lone as incarnate death! O, that the dream
Of dark magician in his visioned cave,
Raking the cinders of a crucible
For life and power, even when his feeble hand
Shakes in its last decay, were the true law
Of this so lovely world! But thou art fled
Like some frail exhalation; which the dawn
Robes in its golden beams,—ah! thou hast fled!
The brave, the gentle, and the beautiful,
The child of grace and genius. Heartless things
Are done and said i' the world, and many worms
And beasts and men live on, and mighty Earth
From sea and mountain, city and wilderness,
In vesper low or joyous orison,
Lifts still its solemn voice:—but thou art fled—

Thou canst no longer know or love the shapes

Of this phantasmal scene, who have to thee

Been purest ministers, who are, alas!

Now thou art not. Upon those pallid lips

So sweet even in their silence, on those eyes

That image sleep in death, upon that form

Yet safe from the worm's outrage, let no tear

Be shed—not even in thought. Nor, when those hues

Are gone, and those divinest lineaments,

Worn by the senseless wind, shall live alone

In the frail pauses of this simple strain,

Let not high verse, mourning the memory

Of that which is no more, or painting's woe

Or sculpture, speak in feeble imagery

Their own cold powers. Art and eloquence,

And all the shows o' the world are frail and vain

To weep a loss that turns their lights to shade.

It is a woe too "deep for tears," when all

Is reft at once, when some surpassing Spirit,

Whose light adorned the world around it, leaves

Those who remain behind, not sobs or groans,

The passionate tumult of a clinging hope;

But pale despair and cold tranquillity,

Nature's vast frame, the web of human things,

Birth and the grave, that are not as they were.

The Cloud

I bring fresh showers for the thirsting flowers,

From the seas and the streams;

I bear light shade for the leaves when laid

In their noonday dreams.

From my wings are shaken the dews that waken

The sweet buds every one,

When rocked to rest on their mother's breast,

As she dances about the sun.

I wield the flail of the lashing hail,

And whiten the green plains under,

And then again I dissolve it in rain,

And laugh as I pass in thunder.

I sift the snow on the mountains below,

And their great pines groan aghast;

And all the night 'tis my pillow white,

While I sleep in the arms of the blast.

Sublime on the towers of my skiey bowers,

Lightning my pilot sits;

In a cavern under is fettered the thunder,

It struggles and howls at fits;

Over earth and ocean, with gentle motion,

This pilot is guiding me,

Lured by the love of the genii that move

In the depths of the purple sea;

Over the rills, and the crags, and the hills,

Over the lakes and the plains,

Wherever he dream, under mountain or stream,

The Spirit he loves remains;

And I all the while bask in Heaven's blue smile,

Whilst he is dissolving in rains.

The sanguine Sunrise, with his meteor eyes,

And his burning plumes outspread,

Leaps on the back of my sailing rack,

When the morning star shines dead;

As on the jag of a mountain crag,

Which an earthquake rocks and swings,

An eagle alit one moment may sit

In the light of its golden wings.

And when Sunset may breathe, from the lit sea beneath,

Its ardours of rest and of love,

And the crimson pall of eve may fall

From the depth of Heaven above,

With wings folded I rest, on mine aëry nest,

As still as a brooding dove.

That orbèd maiden with white fire laden,

Whom mortals call the Moon,

Glides glimmering o'er my fleece-like floor,

By the midnight breezes strewn;

And wherever the beat of her unseen feet,

Which only the angels hear,

May have broken the woof of my tent's thin roof,

The stars peep behind her and peer;

And I laugh to see them whirl and flee,

Like a swarm of golden bees,

When I widen the rent in my wind-built tent,

Till calm the rivers, lakes, and seas,

Like strips of the sky fallen through me on high,

Are each paved with the moon and these.

I bind the Sun's throne with a burning zone,

And the Moon's with a girdle of pearl;

The volcanoes are dim, and the stars reel and swim,

When the whirlwinds my banner unfurl.

From cape to cape, with a bridge-like shape,

Over a torrent sea,

Sunbeam-proof, I hang like a roof,

The mountains its columns be.

The triumphal arch through which I march

With hurricane, fire, and snow,

When the Powers of the air are chained to my chair,

Is the million-coloured bow;

The sphere-fire above its soft colours wove,

While the moist Earth was laughing below.

I am the daughter of Earth and Water,

And the nursling of the Sky;

I pass through the pores of the ocean and shores;

I change, but I cannot die.

For after the rain when with never a stain

The pavilion of Heaven is bare,

And the winds and sunbeams with their convex gleams

Build up the blue dome of air,

I silently laugh at my own cenotaph,

And out of the caverns of rain,

Like a child from the womb, like a ghost from the tomb,

I arise and unbuild it again.

Art thou pale for weariness

Art thou pale for weariness

Of climbing heaven and gazing on the earth,

Wandering companionless

Among the stars that have a different birth,

And ever changing, like a joyless eye

That finds no object worth its constancy?

The Waning Moon

And like a dying lady, lean and pale,

Who totters forth, wrapp'd in a gauzy veil,

Out of her chamber, led by the insane

And feeble wanderings of her fading brain,

The moon arose up in the murky East,

A white and shapeless mass.

Archy's Song from Charles I (A Widow Bird Sate Mourning)

Heigho! the lark and the owl!

One flies the morning, and one lulls the night:

Only the nightingale, poor fond soul,

Sings like the fool through darkness and light.

"A widow bird sate mourning for her love

Upon a wintry bough;

The frozen wind crept on above,

The freezing stream below.

"There was no leaf upon the forest bare,

No flower upon the ground,

And little motion in the air

Except the mill-wheel's sound."

"Ozymandias." *Merriam Webster's Encyclopedia of Literature*, Merriam-Webster, 1995. *Something About the Author*, go.galegroup.com/ps/i.do?p=GLS&sw=w&u=fjp_jvpl&v=2.1&it=r&id=GALE%7CA148921955&asid=54c95dc7f8e03e6d578c1d064650cd29. Accessed date.

Barnhisel, Greg. "Overview of 'For an Assyrian Frieze'." *Poetry for Students*, edited by Ira Mark Milne, vol. 9, Gale, 2000. *Literature Resource Center*, go.galegroup.com/ps/i.do?p=GLS&sw=w&u=fjp_jvpl&v=2.1&it=r&id=GALE%7CH1420031204&asid=2d802ddb093c664cb85ec8d622f03ddc. Accessed date.

Berrigan, Anselm. "Shelley, Percy Bysshe (1729-1822)." *World Poets*, edited by Ron Padgett, vol. 3, Charles Scribner's Sons, 2000, pp. 1-10. *Scribner Writer Series*, go.galegroup.com/ps/i.do?p=GLS&sw=w&u=fjp_jvpl&v=2.1&it=r&id=GALE%7CCX1386400100&asid=59ee5b1c5a00cfd6b6c5a032b8cad32a. Accessed date.

Cummings, Sarah W. "Decadent decay: the complexity of social corruption, consciousness, and critique in Watchmen and You Can't Go Home Again." *Thomas Wolfe Review*, vol. 39, 2015, p. 21+. *Literature Resource Center*, go.galegroup.com/ps/i.do?p=GLS&sw=w&u=fjp_jvpl&v=2.1&it=r&id=GALE%7CA461946463&asid=34ca7aca5efee82eac47af45ca6da6ae. Accessed date.

De Quincey, Thomas. "Percy Bysshe Shelley." *The Works of Thomas De Quincey, vol. 6: Biographical and Historical Essays*, by Thomas De Quincey, vol. 6, Houghton, Mifflin and Company, 1877, p. 290. *LitFinder*, go.galegroup.com/ps/i.do?p=GLS&sw=w&u=fjp_jvpl&v=2.1&it=r&i

d=GALE%7CLTF3000167354WK&asid=e7938ac53cf1ec9fe6da29bcc
23dc532. Accessed date.

Elliott, Brian P. "'Nothing beside remains': Empty Icons and Elegiac
Ekphrasis in Felicia Hemans." *Studies in Romanticism*, vol. 51, no. 1,
2012, p. 25+. *Literature Resource Center*,
go.galegroup.com/ps/i.do?p=GLS&sw=w&u=fjp_jvpl&v=2.1&it=r&i
d=GALE%7CA300061013&asid=63fc72cffdcd372ca8e4ea63cd37bf0
4. Accessed date.

Ferber, Michael. "The Curse of the Ephesians: a long footnote to
Byron." *Byron Journal*, vol. 33, no. 1, 2005, p. 43+. *Literature
Resource Center*,
go.galegroup.com/ps/i.do?p=GLS&sw=w&u=fjp_jvpl&v=2.1&it=r&i
d=GALE%7CA243358304&asid=0bf86b43efeb1e5c0814bd9991d4b
688. Accessed date.

Frank, Kathryn M. "'Who makes the world?': Before watchmen, nostalgia,
and franchising." *Cinema Journal*, vol. 56, no. 2, 2017, p.
138+. *Literature Resource Center*,
go.galegroup.com/ps/i.do?p=GLS&sw=w&u=fjp_jvpl&v=2.1&it=r&i
d=GALE%7CA478824133&asid=f5da146116b6f0f8b9fcf1ef415cc6b
6. Accessed date.

Freedman, William. "Postponement and Perspectives in Shelley's
'Ozymandias'." *Poetry Criticism*, edited by Lawrence J. Trudeau,
vol. 158, Gale, 2014. *Literature Resource Center*,
go.galegroup.com/ps/i.do?p=GLS&sw=w&u=fjp_jvpl&v=2.1&it=r&i
d=GALE%7CH1420118369&asid=ca445974f4ec7b32ea82616176e8
8d1e. Accessed date. Originally published in *Studies in
Romanticism*, vol. 25, no. 1, 1986, pp. 63-73.

Janowitz, Anne. "Shelley's Monument to Ozymandias." *Poetry Criticism*,
edited by Lawrence J. Trudeau, vol. 158, Gale, 2014. *Literature
Resource Center*,
go.galegroup.com/ps/i.do?p=GLS&sw=w&u=fjp_jvpl&v=2.1&it=r&i
d=GALE%7CH1420118368&asid=d0ad40ea308e8f289e3e02d358ee

15d1. Accessed date. Originally published in *Philological Quarterly*, vol. 63, no. 4, 1984, pp. 477-491.

Kinsella, Stuart. "Colonial commemoration in Tudor Ireland: the case of Sir Henry Sidney." *Sidney Journal*, vol. 29, no. 1-2, 2011, p. 105+. *Literature Resource Center*, go.galegroup.com/ps/i.do?p=GLS&sw=w&u=fjp_jvpl&v=2.1&it=r&id=GALE%7CA282068696&asid=3fa86f400b204de98b7d743674cd8a1f. Accessed date.

Lopez, Robert Oscar. "The orientalization of John Winthrop in 'the City in the Sea'." *Gothic Studies*, vol. 12, no. 2, 2010, p. 70+. *Literature Resource Center*, go.galegroup.com/ps/i.do?p=GLS&sw=w&u=fjp_jvpl&v=2.1&it=r&id=GALE%7CA381056571&asid=2112ebf681c004946838e43ee928b2bf. Accessed date.

Lupack, Alan C. "Merlin as New-World Wizard." *Nineteenth-Century Literature Criticism*, edited by Kathy D. Darrow, vol. 204, Gale, 2009. *19th Century Literature Criticism Online*, go.galegroup.com/ps/i.do?p=GLS&sw=w&u=fjp_jvpl&v=2.1&it=r&id=GALE%7CWFOGVR440066889&asid=927cf809ce30cffc87c9fc07a3dcdcc9. Accessed date. Originally published in edited by Peter H. Goodrich and Raymond H. Thompson.

Martin, Karl. "The Love of Nationalism, Internationalism and Sacred Space in *Watchmen*." *Children's Literature Review*, edited by Lawrence J. Trudeau, vol. 209, Gale, 2016. *Literature Resource Center*, go.galegroup.com/ps/i.do?p=GLS&sw=w&u=fjp_jvpl&v=2.1&it=r&id=GALE%7CH1420121866&asid=85d2bf01e9f967a9bc1175ce8f6996fc. Accessed date. Originally published in *Sexual Ideology in the Works of Alan Moore*, edited by Todd A. Comer and Joseph Michael Sommers, McFarland, 2012, pp. 65-74.

O'Dea, Gregory. "Perhaps a Tale You'll Make It: Mary Shelley's Tales for the Keepsake." *Short Story Criticism*, edited by Jelena O. Krstovic, vol. 92, Gale, 2006. *Short Story Criticism Online*, go.galegroup.com/ps/i.do?p=GLS&sw=w&u=fjp_jvpl&v=2.1&it=r&i

d=GALE%7CYBMLYC271583064&asid=aa26e04bbe1bd8090211d0a 5880ea47a. Accessed date. Originally published in *Iconoclastic Departures: Mary Shelley After Frankenstein*, edited by Syndy M. Conger, et al., Farleigh Dickinson University Press, 1997, pp. 62-78.

Parr, Johnstone. "Shelley's *Ozymandias*." *Poetry Criticism*, edited by Lawrence J. Trudeau, vol. 158, Gale, 2014. *Literature Resource Center*, go.galegroup.com/ps/i.do?p=GLS&sw=w&u=fjp_jvpl&v=2.1&it=r&i d=GALE%7CH1420118367&asid=a2f973ac5873facf608cd2690e803 f20. Accessed date. Originally published in *Keats-Shelley Journal*, vol. 6, 1957, pp. 31-35.

Rodenbeck, John. "Travelers from an antique land: Shelley's inspiration for 'Ozymandias'." *Alif: Journal of Comparative Poetics*, no. 24, 2004, p. 121+. *Literature Resource Center*, go.galegroup.com/ps/i.do?p=GLS&sw=w&u=fjp_jvpl&v=2.1&it=r&i d=GALE%7CA126387265&asid=35cf1554484a467be7022f5eb6133 3c7. Accessed date.

Shallcross, Bozena. "Intimations of Intimacy: Adam Mickiewicz's on the Grecian Room." *Nineteenth-Century Literature Criticism*, edited by Thomas J. Schoenberg and Lawrence J. Trudeau, vol. 101, Gale, 2002. *19th Century Literature Criticism Online*, go.galegroup.com/ps/i.do?p=GLS&sw=w&u=fjp_jvpl&v=2.1&it=r&i d=GALE%7CLLYVVT047249241&asid=1a329936f8941eb8c3da948e 8dd172b3. Accessed date. Originally published in *Slavic and Eastern European Journal*, vol. 42, no. 2, Summer 1998, pp. 216-230.

Shelley, Percy Bysshe, and Anna Swanick. "Percy Bysshe Shelley." *Poetry Criticism*, edited by Nancy G. Dziedzic and Christine Slovey, vol. 14, Gale, 1996. *Poetry Criticism Online*, go.galegroup.com/ps/i.do?p=GLS&sw=w&u=fjp_jvpl&v=2.1&it=r&i d=GALE%7CGTZYBP714948006&asid=929c8232268aa05a14f77b0f ddfb30a5. Accessed date. Originally published in *Poets: The Interpreters of Their Age*, George Bell & Sons, 1892, pp. 300-311.

Shelley, Percy Bysshe. "A Defence of Poetry." *Nineteenth-Century Literature Criticism*, edited by Janet Mullane, vol. 18, Gale, 1988. *19th Century Literature Criticism Online*, go.galegroup.com/ps/i.do?p=GLS&sw=w&u=fjp_jvpl&v=2.1&it=r&id=GALE%7CJJYSPD410771674&asid=5b36f0e7e12972c18f44b1acbc9ee019. Accessed date. Originally published in *The Complete Works of Percy Bysshe Shelley: Prose,* by Percy Bysshe Shelley, edited by Roger Ingpen and Walter E. Peck, vol. 7, Gordian Press, 1965, pp. 109-140.

Shelley, Percy Bysshe. "A Preface to Adonais: An Elegy on the Death of John Keats." *Nineteenth-Century Literature Criticism*, edited by Laurie Lanzen Harris, vol. 8, Gale, 1985. *19th Century Literature Criticism Online*, go.galegroup.com/ps/i.do?p=GLS&sw=w&u=fjp_jvpl&v=2.1&it=r&id=GALE%7CHQFSQO133133531&asid=355ca1c3e8bfc8d464ec7b7e8c2211c5. Accessed date. Originally published in *The Complete Poetical Works of Percy Bysshe Shelley*, by Percy Bysshe Shelley, edited by Thomas Hutchinson, Oxford University Press, 1933, pp. 430-431.

Shelley, Percy Bysshe. "Article by Percy Bysshe Shelley." *Shakespearean Criticism*, edited by Laurie Lanzen Harris and Mark W. Scott, vol. 2, Gale, 1985. *Shakespearean Criticism Online*, go.galegroup.com/ps/i.do?p=GLS&sw=w&u=fjp_jvpl&v=2.1&it=r&id=GALE%7CLLGNZY340512580&asid=f5e79d1fbaa91b6e01155c16ae56ee72. Accessed date. Originally published in *A Defence of Poetry*, by Percy Bysshe Shelley, edited by Shelley, The Bobbs-Merrill Company, 1904.

Shelley, Percy Bysshe. "Essay on the Literature, the Arts, and the Manners of the Athenians." *A Defence of Poetry and Other Essays*, by Percy Bysshe Shelley, ICON Classics, 2008, pp. 45-51. *LitFinder*, go.galegroup.com/ps/i.do?p=GLS&sw=w&u=fjp_jvpl&v=2.1&it=r&id=GALE%7CCX3330500012&asid=3f8f0d6945a88d4b6eb9283dd98871b9. Accessed date.

Shelley, Percy Bysshe. "In a letter to Lord Byron dated October 21, 1821." *Poetry Criticism*, edited by Margaret Haerens and Christine Slovey, vol. 16, Gale, 1997. *Literature Resource Center*, go.galegroup.com/ps/i.do?p=GLS&sw=w&u=fjp_jvpl&v=2.1&it=r&id=GALE%7CH1420011751&asid=437e8a7c51126e108678f3b2022faa63. Accessed date. Originally published in *The Letters of Percy Bysshe Shelley, Vol. II: Shelley in Italy*, edited by Frederick L. Jones, Oxford at the Clarendon Press, 1964, pp. 357-359.

Shelley, Percy Bysshe. "In a Letter to Mrs. Shelley on August 20, 1818." *Shakespearean Criticism*, edited by Mark W. Scott and Sandra L. Williamson, vol. 9, Gale, 1989. *Shakespearean Criticism Online*, go.galegroup.com/ps/i.do?p=GLS&sw=w&u=fjp_jvpl&v=2.1&it=r&id=GALE%7CGPTCNN572078149&asid=81e46cb3e592926070e582d8ae533636. Accessed date. Originally published in *Essays,Letters from Abroad, Translations and Fragments*, by Percy Bysshe Shelley, edited by Mrs. Shelley and Edward Moxon, vol. 2, 1840, pp. 130-134.

Shelley, Percy Bysshe. "In a Preface to Adonais: An Elegy on the Death of John Keats." *Nineteenth-Century Literature Criticism*, edited by Laurie Lanzen Harris, vol. 10, Gale, 1985. *19th Century Literature Criticism Online*, go.galegroup.com/ps/i.do?p=GLS&sw=w&u=fjp_jvpl&v=2.1&it=r&id=GALE%7CIPPIEH060927555&asid=1383a840c02eea1fc8c6483fb7c9bd36. Accessed date. Originally published in *Adonais*, by Percy Bysshe Shelley, edited by William Michael Rossetti, Oxford at the Clarendon Press, 1891, pp. 69-71.

Shelley, Percy Bysshe. "On Life." *A Defence of Poetry and Other Essays*, by Percy Bysshe Shelley, ICON Classics, 2008, pp. 5-9. *LitFinder*, go.galegroup.com/ps/i.do?p=GLS&sw=w&u=fjp_jvpl&v=2.1&it=r&id=GALE%7CCX3330500007&asid=f7d188e767813ef9950bae1f2e0b95c3. Accessed date.

Shelley, Percy Bysshe. "On Love." *A Defence of Poetry and Other Essays*, by Percy Bysshe Shelley, ICON Classics, 2008, pp. 2-4. *LitFinder*,

go.galegroup.com/ps/i.do?p=GLS&sw=w&u=fjp_jvpl&v=2.1&it=r&i
d=GALE%7CCX3330500006&asid=7a68e2f62ec0cd73cfc3b7a939b0
799c. Accessed date.

Shelley, Percy Bysshe. "On the Devil, and Devils." *Literature Criticism from 1400 to 1800*, edited by James E. Person, Jr., vol. 9, Gale, 1989. *Literature Resource Center*, go.galegroup.com/ps/i.do?p=GLS&sw=w&u=fjp_jvpl&v=2.1&it=r&i d=GALE%7CH1420016689&asid=9029fd45b5623b30c1518a13ba41 a157. Accessed date. Originally published in *The Prose Works of Percy Bysshe Shelley*, edited by Harry Buxton Forman, 1876.

Shelley, Percy Bysshe. "Speculations on Metaphysics." *A Defence of Poetry and Other Essays*, by Percy Bysshe Shelley, ICON Classics, 2008, pp. 23-30. *LitFinder*, go.galegroup.com/ps/i.do?p=GLS&sw=w&u=fjp_jvpl&v=2.1&it=r&i d=GALE%7CCX3330500010&asid=6dab771cabf37bafabe2576da9f5 6b93. Accessed date.

Shelley, Percy Bysshe. "The Revolt of Islam." *Nineteenth-Century Literature Criticism*, edited by Jay Parini, vol. 14, Gale, 1987. *19th Century Literature Criticism Online*, go.galegroup.com/ps/i.do?p=GLS&sw=w&u=fjp_jvpl&v=2.1&it=r&i d=GALE%7CINFWRK541481441&asid=723e705a17f01893054cb2d d6c351f5d. Accessed date. Originally published in *Poetical Works*, by Percy Bysshe Shelley, edited by Thomas Hutchinson and G. M. Matthews, Oxford University Press, 1970, pp. 31-158.

Sorensen, Peter. "New Light on Shelley's 'Ozymandias': Shelley as Prophet of the 'New Israel.'." *Nineteenth-Century Literature Criticism*, edited by Kathy D. Darrow, vol. 204, Gale, 2009. *Literature Resource Center*, go.galegroup.com/ps/i.do?p=GLS&sw=w&u=fjp_jvpl&v=2.1&it=r&i d=GALE%7CH1420087306&asid=aa19ea6e4fbf8a9eeecfee2ec7f92 9e6. Accessed date. Originally published in *Keats-Shelley Review*, vol. 16, 2002, pp. 74-93.

Sorensen, Peter. "New Light on Shelley's Ozymandias: Shelley As Prophet of the New Israel." *Nineteenth-Century Literature Criticism*, edited by Kathy D. Darrow, vol. 204, Gale, 2009. *19th Century Literature Criticism Online*, go.galegroup.com/ps/i.do?p=GLS&sw=w&u=fjp_jvpl&v=2.1&it=r&id=GALE%7CUKHFEQ557741950&asid=1cc15b74282dd40a1ab6f319ef2ae7b3. Accessed date. Originally published in *Keats-Shelley Review*, vol. 16, 2002, pp. 74-93.

Sperry, Stuart M. "The Ethical Politics of Shelley's *The Cenci*." *Nineteenth-Century Literature Criticism*, edited by Russel Whitaker, vol. 143, Gale, 2005. *Literature Resource Center*, go.galegroup.com/ps/i.do?p=GLS&sw=w&u=fjp_jvpl&v=2.1&it=r&id=GALE%7CH1420059961&asid=5988851e7be02155d548772db680ed2d. Accessed date. Originally published in *Studies in Romanticism*, vol. 25, no. 3, Fall 1986, pp. 411-427.

Spiegelman, Willard. "Alphabetizing the Void: Poetic Diction and Poetic Classicism." *Twentieth-Century Literary Criticism*, edited by Janet Witalec, vol. 124, Gale, 2002. *Literature Resource Center*, go.galegroup.com/ps/i.do?p=GLS&sw=w&u=fjp_jvpl&v=2.1&it=r&id=GALE%7CH1420046450&asid=6ed12e53e438861ffafe03998e327dfe. Accessed date. Originally published in *Salmagundi*, vol. 42, 1978, pp. 132-145.

Wagner-Lawlor, Jennifer A. "A Figure of Resistance: The Visionary Reader in Shelley's Sonnets and the 'West Wind' Ode." *Poetry Criticism*, edited by Lawrence J. Trudeau, vol. 161, Gale, 2015. *Literature Resource Center*, go.galegroup.com/ps/i.do?p=GLS&sw=w&u=fjp_jvpl&v=2.1&it=r&id=GALE%7CH1420118744&asid=08f18ec17bea1122a2c37c0638583545. Accessed date. Originally published in *Southwest Review*, vol. 77, no. 1, 1992, pp. 109-127.

Waith, Eugene M. "Ozymandias: Shelley, Horace Smith, and Denon." *Keats-Shelley Journal* 44 (1995): 22-28.